This book is a presentation of Weekly Reader
Books. Weekly Reader Books offers book
clubs for children from preschool through high
school. For further information write to:
WEEKLY READER BOOKS, 4343 Equity Drive,
Columbus, Ohio 43228

This edition is published by arrangement
with Checkerboard Press.

Weekly Reader Books offers several exciting
card and activity programs. For more information,
write to WEEKLY READER BOOKS, P.O. Box 16636
Columbus, Ohio 43216.

WEEKLY READER BOOKS presents

What Is a Rainbow?

A **Just Ask**™ Book

by Chris Arvetis
and Carole Palmer

illustrated by
James Buckley

FIELD PUBLICATIONS
MIDDLETOWN, CT.

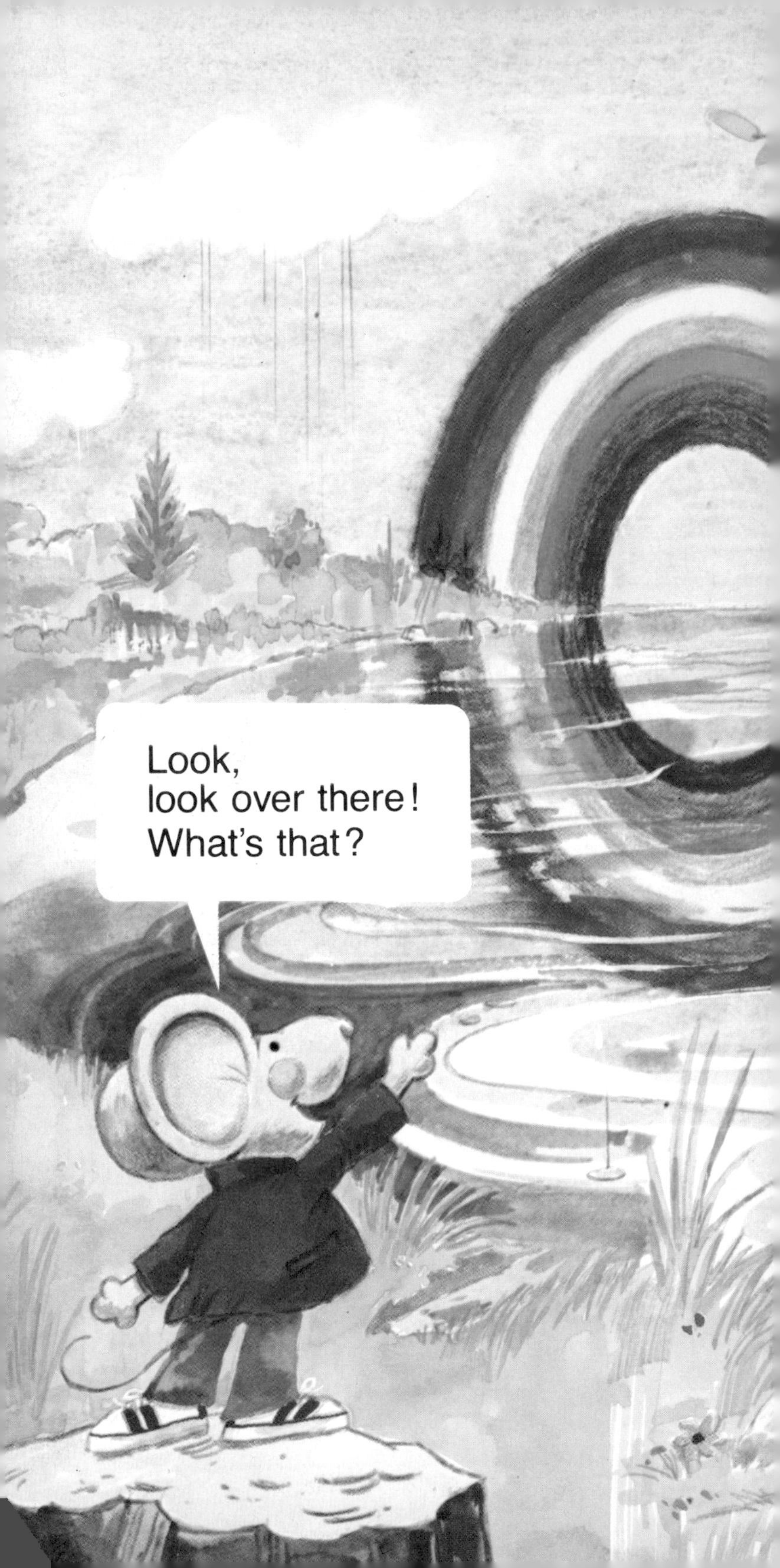
Look, look over there! What's that?

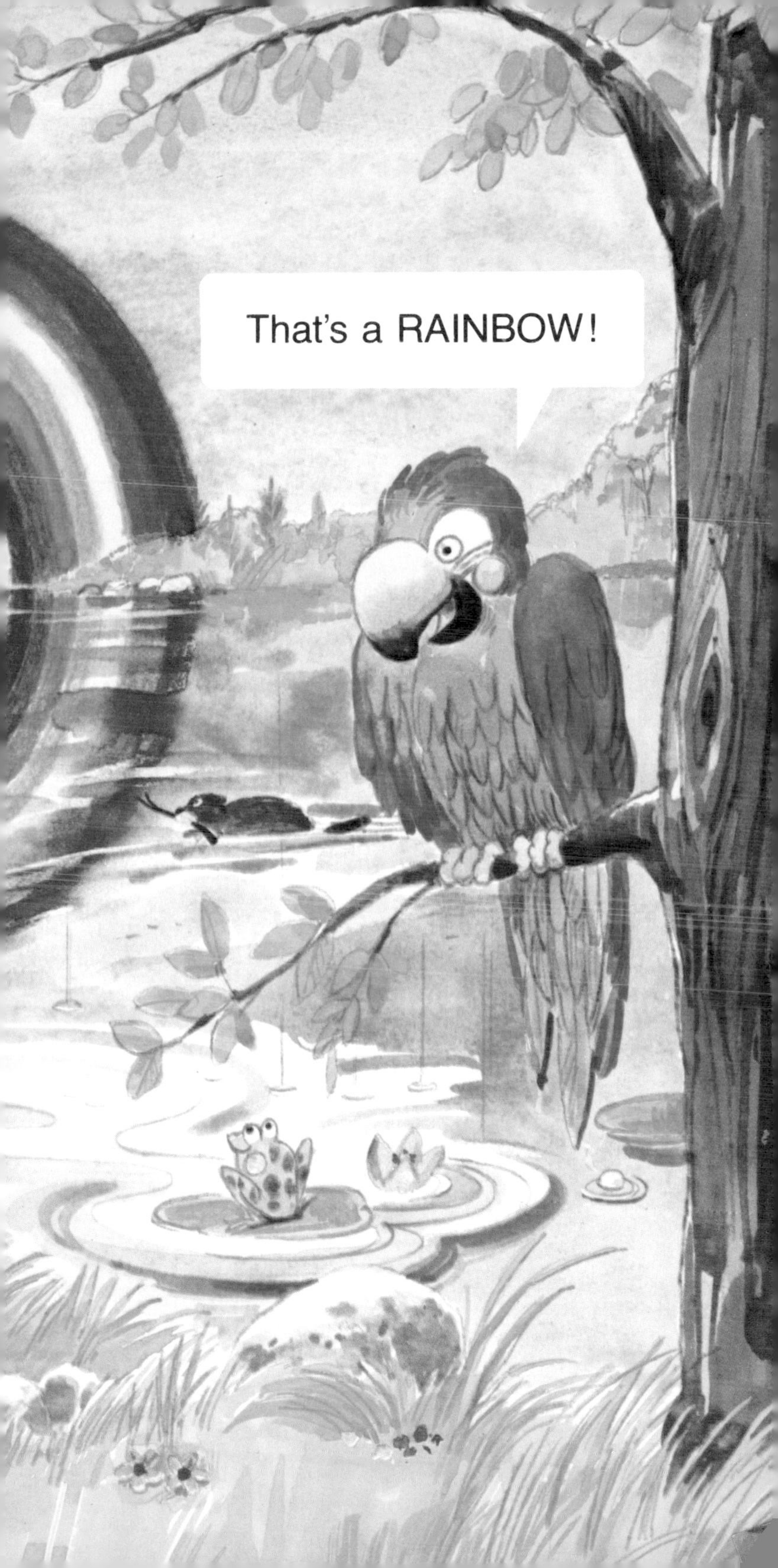
That's a RAINBOW!

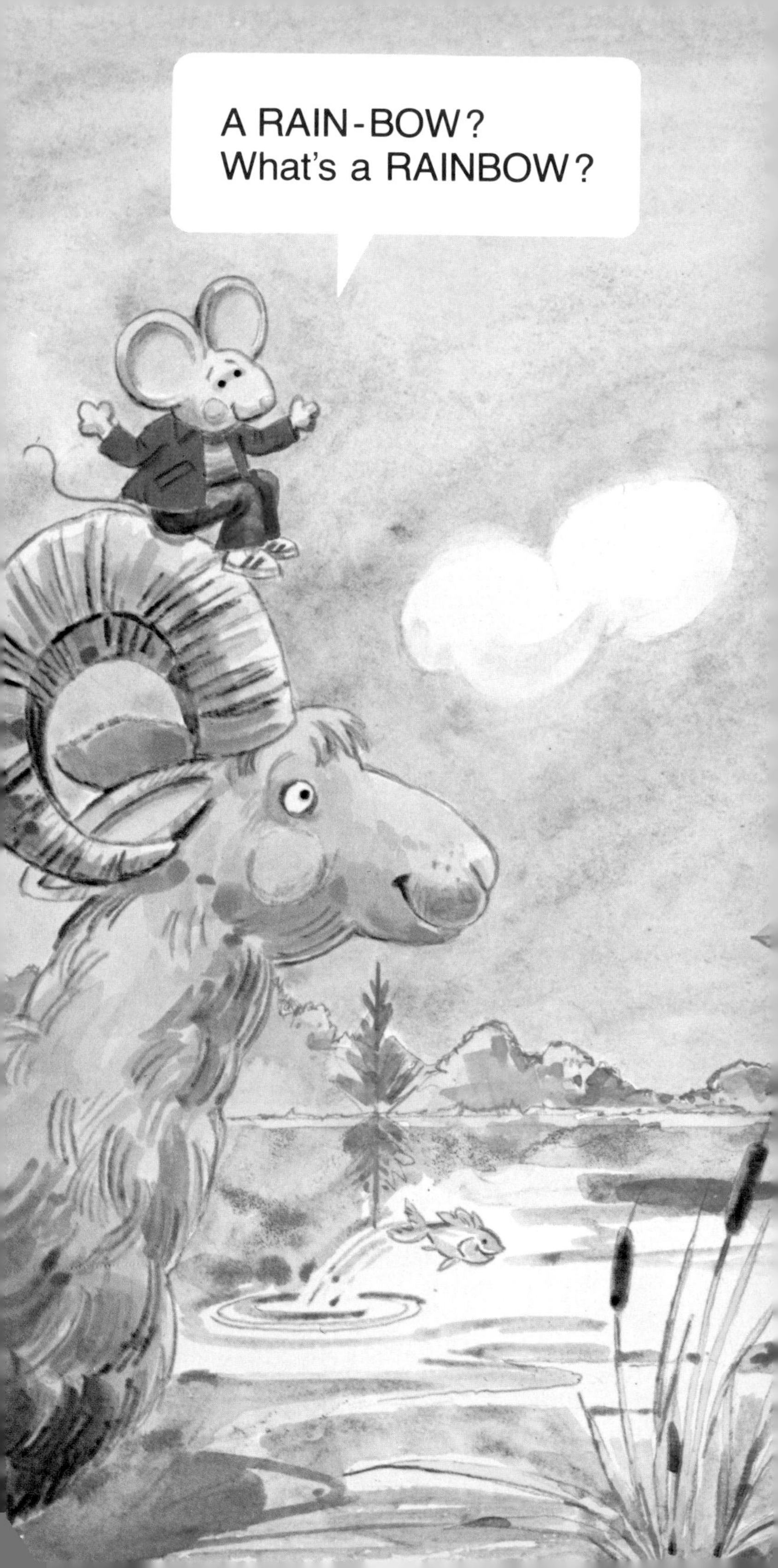
A RAIN-BOW?
What's a RAINBOW?

That's
an interesting
question.
Maybe Beaver
can help us.

Hi, Beaver!
Can you help us?
What makes a rainbow?

Well, let me
show you.

See this? This is called a PRISM. It is made of glass. Let's say it together – PRISM.
Prism!

As the sun's rays
shine through the prism,
the light is bent.
As the light bends,
it splits into many colors.

In the sunlight
there are many colors.

The same thing happens
when the sunlight shines
through the rain.
Let's go to the waterfall
and I'll show you.

Interesting!

The light from the sun shines through the water. The drops of water are like tiny prisms.

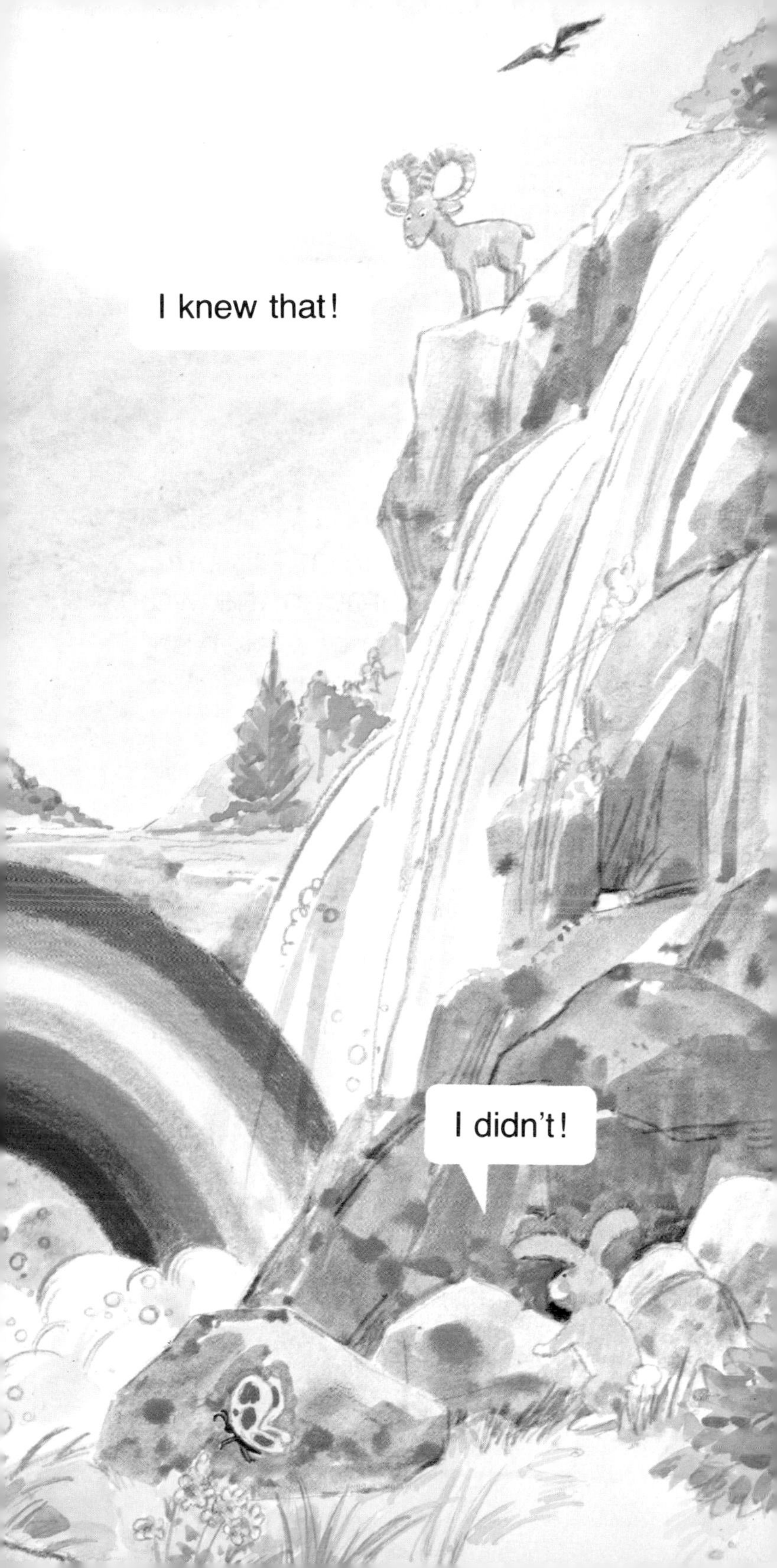
I knew that!
I didn't!

As the drops of water bend the light, we see the many colors of the rainbow.

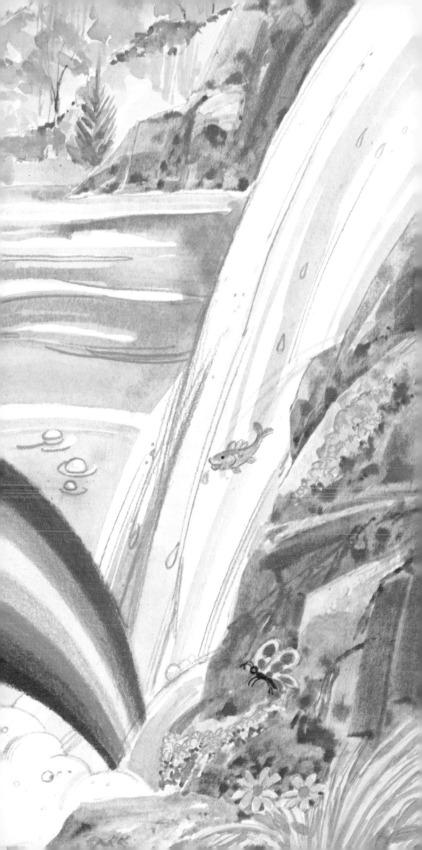

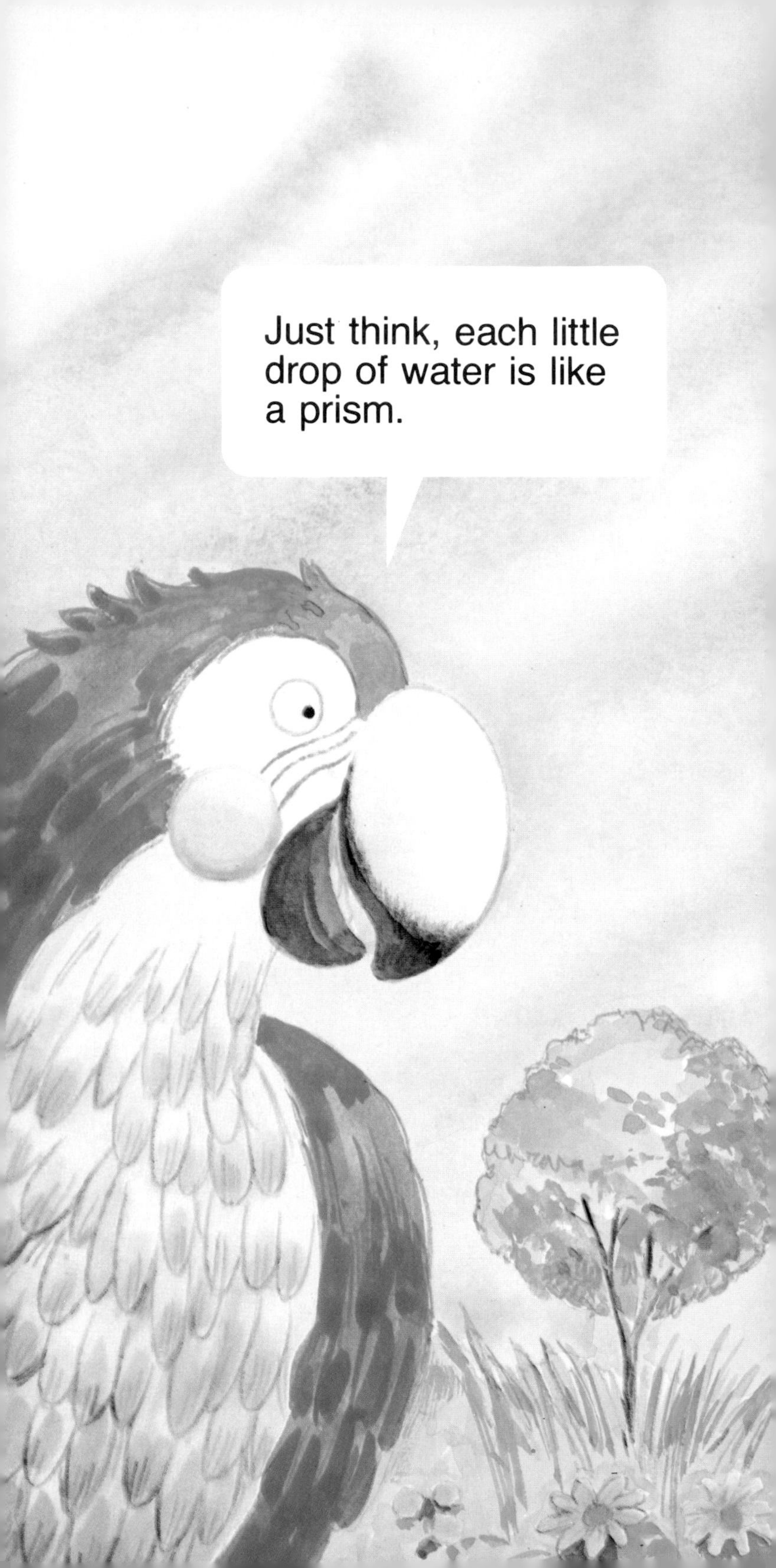
Just think, each little drop of water is like a prism.

Let's go up into the sky
and look at the rainbow.

See how bright the sun
is shining.
The air is full of drops
of water from the rain.

The sunlight shines
through the drops.
The raindrops are
like tiny prisms.
They bend the sunlight
and split it into many colors.

As we look
into the sky,
we see – –

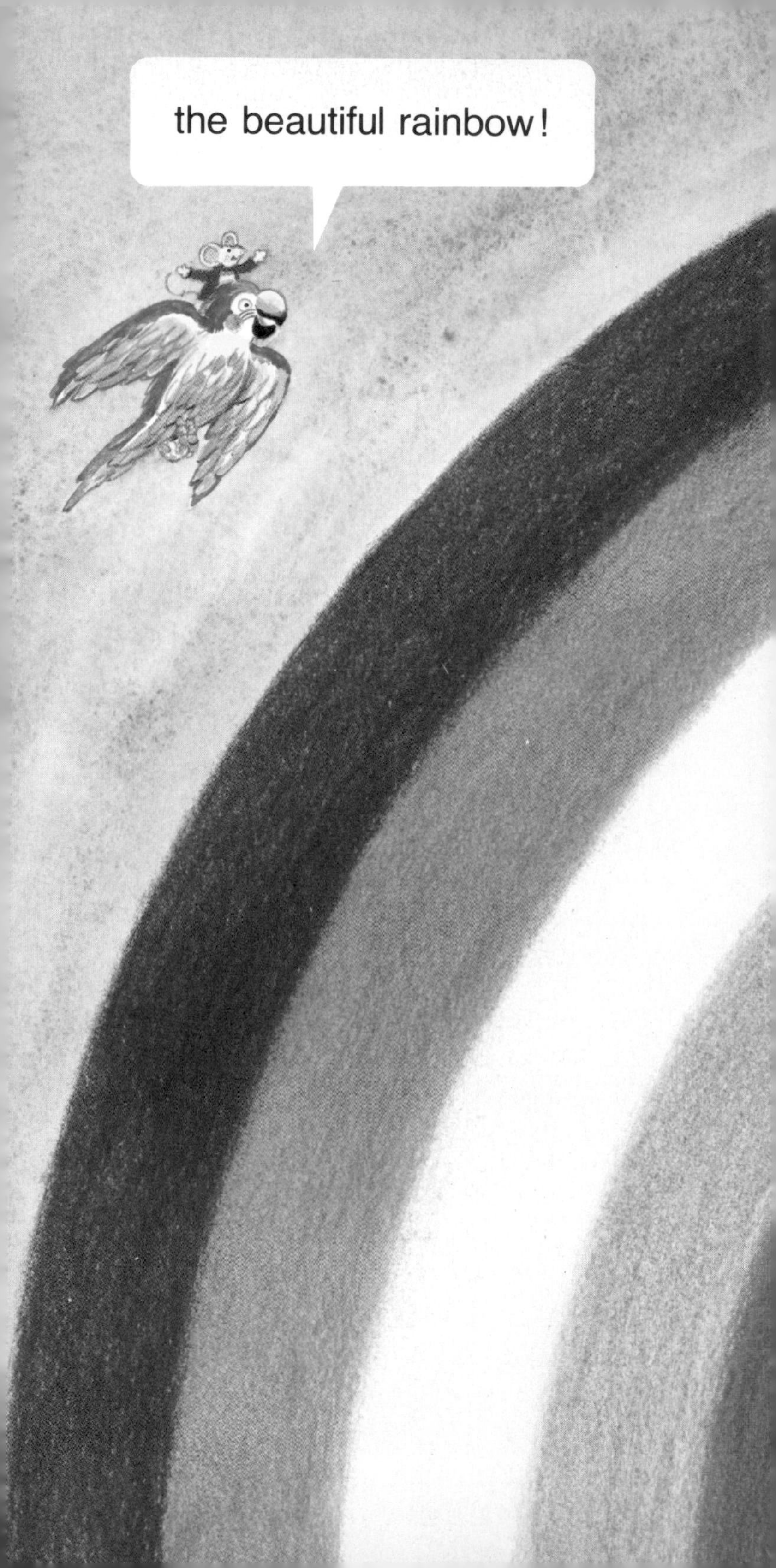
the beautiful rainbow!

Me too!

We do too!

Now I know
what makes
a rainbow!